How to talk to Anybody

master the skills to connect,
influence, and thrive in every
conversation

Dr. John K. Moore

Table of Contents

Introduction

Mark found himself at a crossroads in the city's busy core, where the noise of activity rang across congested streets. His professional existence necessitated networking, and his personal life desired deeper ties, but every effort at conversation left him feeling like a passenger on a sinking ship.

Mark came upon a treasure titled "How to Talk to Anyone" while browsing through the enormous sea of self-help books one day. He dived into its pages with interest, skeptical but anxious for change. He had no idea that this book would be the trigger for a life-changing voyage.

Mark encountered communication complexities he had never considered before as he immersed himself in the knowledge inside. The fundamentals of successful talks were evident, and the art of nonverbal signs blossomed like a secret language. He learned to sculpt his words with thought and skill with each chapter, converting his verbal expression into a strong instrument.

The true breakthrough occurred when Mark confronted the intimidating realm of small conversation. He found himself readily beginning discussions and turning casual meetings into significant friendships once armed with novel methods. His social scene transformed, and his coworkers noticed—a more confident, engaged Mark had emerged.

His superpower became active listening. He absorbed material like a sponge in meetings, answering wisely and creating rapport. Mark was able to negotiate issues with diplomacy and escape unhurt from the once-tough domain of unpleasant discussions.

Mark's personal life flourished in addition to his business life. The book's insights for strengthening ties aided him in creating genuine relationships. Networking gatherings became opportunities for actual interaction, and his social circle grew.

Mark's knowledge of cultural communication also evolved. He valued variety and handled cross-cultural interactions with elegance and respect.

The city, which was previously a maze of isolated lives, transformed into a tapestry of shared experiences.

Mark seamlessly navigated virtual chats and crafted an online persona that mirrored his increased communication ability in the digital age. The previously timid guy has developed into a master communicator.

Mark's transformation was not unnoticed. Friends and coworkers were astounded by his metamorphosis and wanted to know the key to his newfound magnetism. Mark would suggest the book that had opened the door to a world of efficient communication with a grin.

"How to Talk to Anyone" was not simply a book for him; it was the key that unlocked a lifetime of meaningful interactions and limitless prospects.

Chapter 1: The Foundations of Great Conversations

Understanding the Dynamics of Communication

The process of communicating information, ideas, sentiments, and emotions with others is known as communication. It is a necessary talent for forming connections, expressing ourselves, and attaining our objectives. Communication can be vocal or nonverbal, oral or written, formal or informal, deliberate or inadvertent, and formal or casual.

The aspects that determine how communication happens, such as the context, the participants, the message, the channel, the feedback, and the noise, are referred to as communication dynamics. Understanding these dynamics can aid in more efficient communication and the avoidance of misconceptions.

The scenario or environment in which communication takes place is referred to as the context. It covers the physical, social, cultural, historical, and psychological factors that influence the message's meaning and interpretation. A chat between two friends in a coffee shop, for example, is not the same as a presentation at a conference. The tone, style, and content of communication are influenced by the setting.

Participants: The persons who are participating in the communication process, either as message senders or receivers, are referred to as participants. Participants have diverse roles, expectations, objectives, values, views, attitudes, emotions, and personalities, which influence how they communicate and how others communicate. For example, in a negotiation between a buyer and a seller, the players' interests and views impact their communication techniques and outcomes.

The message is the information, concept, sentiment, or emotion that the sender communicates to the receiver. The communication might be spoken or written, verbal or nonverbal, and can include words, symbols, gestures, emotions, or noises.

The message has two components: content and format. The substance of the message is the actual information or meaning of the communication, whereas the form is how the message is conveyed or displayed. For example, depending on the situation and participants, the message "I love you" might have distinct substance and form. The message can be delivered orally or nonverbally, seriously or ironically, loudly or quietly, and so on.

The channel is the medium or mechanism via which the communication is transferred from sender to receiver. Face-to-face contact, phone conversations, emails, texts, social media, letters, books, films, and other forms of communication are examples of channels.

The channel influences the message's speed, accuracy, and clarity, as well as the feedback and interaction between participants. Face-to-face contact, for example, provides rapid feedback and nonverbal clues, but email communication may generate delays and misconceptions.

Feedback: The receiver's response or reaction to the sender's message is referred to as feedback. Feedback can be spoken or nonverbal, positive or negative, direct or indirect, and might reflect the receiver's degree of comprehension, agreement, interest, or contentment. The feedback allows the sender to assess the success of the communication and alter the message as needed.

A grin, a nod, or a question, for example, might demonstrate the receiver's gratitude, comprehension, or curiosity about the message.

Noise: Any component that interferes with or distorts the communication process is referred to as noise. Noise can be physical, psychological, semantic, or cultural, and it can come from the sender, receiver, message, channel, or environment. Noise from loud music, a distracting idea, a confused term, a weak connection, or a foreign culture, for example, can all impede communication and lead to misunderstandings or errors.

We may improve our communication abilities and our connections with others by understanding the mechanics of communication. We can also prevent or overcome any roadblocks and problems in the communication process. In the next chapter, we will look at the concepts and techniques of successful communication, as well as how to use them in various settings and contexts.

Building Genuine Interest and Empathy

The capacity to demonstrate real attention and empathy for the other person is one of the most critical abilities for having successful discussions. Genuine attention and empathy are more than polite gestures or surface praises.

They are genuine displays of interest, admiration, and comprehension that make the other person feel appreciated, respected and heard.

Genuine interest and empathy can be exhibited in a variety of ways, including:

Inviting the other person to disclose more about themselves, their thoughts, their feelings, and their experiences by asking open-ended questions. Instead of raising the question, "Do you like your job?" you may ask, "What do you like best about your job?" or "How did you become inquisitive in your field?"

Actively and intently listening to the replies of others without interrupting, judging, or changing the issue. Nod, make eye contact, and provide a vocal response such as "Uh-huh", "I see", or "That's interesting" to demonstrate that you are listening.

Reflecting on what the other person said, either by paraphrasing or summarizing, to demonstrate understanding and verify for correctness. As an illustration, you may say: "So, what you're saying is that you discern frustrated by the lack of communication in your team" or "Let me see if I got this right: you love traveling because it gives you a sense of adventure and freedom".

Demonstrating empathy by acknowledging the other person's feelings and validating their point of view. Empathic remarks such as "I can imagine how you feel" "That must have been difficult for you" or "I understand why you think that way" might be used. Empathic gestures such as smiling, nodding, or stroking the other person's arm or shoulder (if suitable) can also be used.

- Sharing something about yourself that corresponds to what the other person stated, to demonstrate that you have something in common with them or that you understand their predicament. For example, you may say "I know how you feel, I had an identical understanding when I ..." instead of "That's hilarious, I also like ..." instead of "That's amazing, I've always wanted to ...".

Appreciating and thanking the other person for their time, attention, and participation in the discourse. You can say something like, "Thank you for sharing that with me," "I enjoyed talking to you," or "You gave me a lot to think about." You may also utilize gestures like shaking hands, embracing, or complimenting.

By demonstrating real attention and empathy, you may establish a good and meaningful relationship with the other person, increasing their likelihood of opening up, trusting you, and enjoying the discussion. You may also uncover fresh ideas, views, and possibilities by learning more about them, their beliefs, ambitions, and issues.

Genuine curiosity and empathy are the building blocks of successful talks, and they may strengthen both your personal and professional relationships.

Chapter 2: Mastering Non-Verbal Communication

The Language of Body: Gestures, Posture, and Eye Contact

Nonverbal communication is an important part of every discussion since it may express messages that words cannot. The language of the body relates to how we express ourselves, affect others, and understand their messages through gestures, posture, and eye contact. Depending on how we utilize it, body language may either enhance or detract from our spoken communication.

Gestures are the hand, arm, head, and facial motions that accompany human speech. Gestures can be used for a variety of purposes, including:

- Use gestures to emphasize or illustrate our arguments, such as pointing, nodding, or shaking our heads.
- Raise our hand, wave, or snap our fingers to control the flow of the talk.
- Smiling, frowning, or shrugging to express our emotions, attitudes, or intentions.
- Thumbs up, OK sign, or peace sign can be used to replace words, especially when we are in a noisy or remote setting.
- When we communicate, we posture and hold our bodies in certain ways.

Our posture may represent our confidence, curiosity, and openness, as well as our mood, vitality, and health. Several variables can impact posture, including:

- The distance that separates us from the other person, might show our level of closeness, comfort, and respect.
- Our body's orientation might indicate our level of attention, participation, and alignment with the other person.
- Our body's symmetry and balance might show our level of relaxation, stability, and harmony.
- When we communicate, we make eye contact by staring at the other person's eyes.

Our degree of interest, attentiveness, and honesty, as well as our emotions, ideas, and desires, may all be communicated through eye contact. Several variables can influence eye contact, including:

Our gaze's duration might show our level of attention, attraction, or dominance.

The frequency with which weblink might indicate our level of tension, anxiousness, or boredom.

Our gaze's direction might show our level of attention, interest, or distraction.

The language of the body is a tremendous tool for improving our communication abilities and relationships.

However, body language is not universal, and it can differ based on culture, circumstance, and particular preferences of those involved.

As a result, it is critical to be aware of the many meanings and interpretations of our gestures, posture, and eye contact, and to adjust them to the circumstance and the person with whom we are conversing. We may then utilize body language to communicate more effectively, convincingly, and politely.

Unleashing the Power of Facial Expressions

One of the most expressive and influential kinds of nonverbal communication is facial expression. The movements and configurations of our facial muscles that reflect our emotions, moods, and attitudes are referred to as facial expressions.

Our intentions, expectations, and emotions to the other person and the event may also be communicated through facial expressions.

There are two sorts of facial expressions: universal and culturally distinctive. Happiness, sorrow, anger, fear, surprise, and disgust are examples of universal facial emotions that are recognized and understood across cultures and settings.

Culture-specific facial expressions are those that are impacted by a given culture's or group's norms, values, and conventions, such as respect, disdain, shame, or pride.

Facial expressions have a big influence on our communication and relationships since they can:

Enhance or contradict our spoken signals by smiling or frowning when we say anything pleasant or bad.

We can exaggerate or moderate our emotions by enlarging our eyes when we are excited or biting our lower lip when we are scared.

Raise our brows when we are intrigued or yawn when we are bored to signal or manage our interest and attentiveness.
Influence or convince the other person by nodding or shaking our heads when we agree or disagree.

Mirroring the other person's facial expressions or exhibiting scorn or disgust can build or shatter rapport and trust.
Facial expressions are an important technique for communicating more effectively, genuinely, and empathically.

Facial expressions, on the other hand, are not always easy to regulate, interpret, or adjust since they can be impacted by a variety of events, including:

The communication setting and intent might influence the appropriateness, intensity, and frequency of our facial expressions.

The other person's culture and background might influence the meaning, expectation, and interpretation of our facial expressions. Our and the other person's personality and mood might influence expression, recognition, and response to our facial expressions.

The other person's input and reaction might influence the adjustment, reinforcement, or inhibition of our facial expressions.

As a result, it is critical to understand the power and hazards of facial expressions, as well as how to utilize them wisely and successfully. By doing so, we may harness the power of facial expressions to better our communication and relationships.

Chapter 3: Crafting Your Verbal Expression

The Art of Articulation: Clarity and Precision

The art of articulation is one of the most important abilities for efficient communication. Articulation refers to the capacity to convey your thoughts, ideas, and opinions clearly and exactly, utilizing suitable, correct, and meaningful language. Articulation can assist you in:

Without being imprecise, ambiguous, or confusing, communicate your point with confidence and authority. Engage and convince your audience while being interesting, repetitious, and current.

Avoid miscommunications and disputes by not being hostile, defensive, or deceptive.

Articulation entails not just selecting the appropriate words, but also structuring them logically and clearly. To master the art of articulation, one must first understand several fundamental concepts, such as:

Understand your goal and your target audience. Before you speak or write, you should know exactly what you want to say and why you want to express it. You should also think about who you're talking to and what they need to know, understand, or do. This will assist you in tailoring your message to your aim and audience.

To explain complicated thoughts, use simple words. You may need to explain a complicated subject, procedure, or problem to your audience at times. Instead of jargon, technical phrases, or esoteric language, employ straightforward and common words that your audience will comprehend. Analogies, metaphors, and examples can also be used to demonstrate your idea and make it more approachable.

Break difficult topics down into simple frameworks and models. Another method for simplifying complicated ideas is to divide them into smaller and simpler sections and demonstrate how they are interrelated and related.

Frameworks and models may be used to arrange your material into categories, processes, stages, or components, as well as to demonstrate the cause and effect, pros and drawbacks, or similarities and contrasts between your thoughts.

Be specific and exact. When communicating, avoid using phrases that are vague, generic, or ambiguous since they might have several meanings or interpretations. Instead, use explicit and precise terms that express exactly what you intend and desire. You may also utilize data, facts, or proof to back up your statements and demonstrate the scope, scale, or significance of your views.

Keep it short and to the point. When communicating, avoid using too many words, phrases, or paragraphs, which might lengthen, bore, or confuse your message. Instead, employ just the words, phrases, or paragraphs that are required, relevant, and important to your message. Transitions, headers, and bullet points can also be used to arrange your message and highlight the major points and vital themes.

By adhering to these guidelines, you will be able to master the art of articulation and convey your thoughts, ideas, and opinions clearly and accurately. Articulation may help you enhance your personal and professional relationships by allowing you to speak more effectively, convincingly, and politely.

Harnessing the Strength of Tone and Pitch

The capacity to employ tone and pitch to improve verbal expression is another crucial skill for efficient communication. The changes in your voice that reflect your emotions, attitudes, and intentions are known as tone and pitch. Tone and pitch can also impact your audience's emotions, attitudes, and intentions.

The character or emotion of your voice, such as warm, frigid, friendly, unfriendly, calm, or angry, is referred to as tone. Tone may express your sentiments and ideas about the issue, circumstance, or person you're speaking with. Tone may also influence how your audience perceives and receives your message.

Pitch refers to the highness or lowness of your voice, which can be expressed as high, low, rising, or falling. Pitch may express your amount of certainty, uncertainty, or query, as well as your level of confidence, curiosity, and enthusiasm. Pitch may also have an impact on how your message is conveyed and received by your audience.

Tone and pitch are significant tools that can help you do the following:

Without becoming monotonic, uninteresting, or robotic, express oneself more sincerely and strongly.

Engage and convince your audience more successfully and convincingly, without coming across as dull, bland, or uninterested.

Without being harsh, confrontational, or sarcastic, avoid misunderstandings and disputes more quickly and pleasantly.

To master the use of tone and pitch, you must first follow certain fundamental criteria, such as:

Understand your goal and your target audience. Before you talk, you should know exactly what you want to accomplish and who you want to reach.

You should also think about the context and surroundings of your speech. This will assist you in tailoring your tone and pitch to your purpose and audience.

To portray your emotions and attitudes, use tone. When you talk, choose a tone that reflects your feelings and attitudes, and that clearly and truly delivers your message. You should also adopt an acceptable and courteous tone for the situation and the person you are speaking with. When greeting someone, for example, you may adopt a warm and pleasant tone, a quiet and soothing tone when comforting someone, or a forceful and authoritative tone while making a request.

Pitch to show your confidence and interest. When you talk, you should adopt a pitch that conveys your confidence and interest while also successfully and convincingly delivering your message. You should also select a pitch that is appropriate for your voice and your audience. When asking a question, for example, you may use a high and rising pitch, a low and falling pitch when making a remark, or a varied and modulated pitch when telling a narrative.

Chapter 4: Breaking the Ice and Initiating Conversations

Strategies for Confident Introductions

Making a good first impression is one of the most difficult elements of socializing. How do you approach a stranger or introduce yourself to someone you don't know? How do you prevent awkward silences while being confident and friendly?

Mentally and emotionally prepare yourself.
It is critical to mentally and emotionally prepare oneself before approaching someone. This will assist you in reducing worry, increasing confidence, and increasing your chances of success. Here are some measures you may take to get ready:

Set a specific and attainable aim. What do you want to accomplish by speaking with this person? Do you want to meet a new acquaintance, develop a business contact, find a romantic companion, or simply have a casual conversation? A specific and attainable objective can help you focus your attention and energy while avoiding unwarranted expectations or pressure. Instead of thinking, "I want to impress this person and make them like me," consider, "I want to have a friendly and interesting conversation with this person and see if we have anything in common."

Conduct some research. Before approaching someone, attempt to learn as much as you can about them or the circumstance.

This will allow you to personalize your introduction and icebreaker to their specific hobbies, history, or requirements. For example, if you are attending a networking event, you can look up the speakers' or attendees' profiles on LinkedIn or the event website. If you meet someone through a common acquaintance, you can ask your buddy for some background information about them.

If you approach a stranger in a public setting, you might look for indications in their appearance, demeanor, or surroundings. Doing some study will help you avoid improper or irrelevant issues while also demonstrating your interest and respect.

Reframe your thinking. How you see yourself and the environment will influence how you feel and behave. You will feel more frightened, uneasy, and discouraged if you hold negative or limiting thoughts such as "I'm not good enough", "I have nothing to offer", "They will reject me", or "This is too hard". Instead, attempt to reset your mentality and embrace positive and powerful ideas like "I'm worthy of respect", "I have something valuable to share", "They will appreciate my effort", or "This is a learning opportunity". You will feel more confident, optimistic, and resilient after reframing your perspective.

To communicate confidence and curiosity, use body language, eye contact, and voice tone.

When approaching someone, nonverbal communication is as crucial as verbal communication. Your body language, eye contact, and voice tone may express both confidence and indifference. Here are some pointers on how to make the most of your nonverbal communication:

Maintain an open and easygoing body language. Crossing your arms, slouching, or fidgeting are all signs of uneasiness, defensiveness, or boredom. Instead, utilize open and comfortable body language, such as standing or sitting up straight, smiling, nodding, and leaning forward gently.

These actions can convey confidence, warmth, and attention.

Maintain eye contact but do not stare. One of the most potent methods to create rapport and trust with someone is through eye contact. It demonstrates that you are interested and involved in the discourse. Too much eye contact, on the other hand, can be threatening or creepy, while too little eye contact can be impolite or distant. The best amount of eye contact varies based on culture and context, but a basic rule of thumb is to keep eye contact for around 60% of the time, with breaks for looking at something else or blinking. This will naturally and comfortably build a balance of connection and respect.

Speak in a clear and expressive tone of voice. The tone of your voice may reflect your emotions, attitudes, and objectives. A clear and expressive voice tone can convey confidence, enthusiasm, and sincerity, whereas a muffled, monotonous, or hesitant voice tone might convey insecurity, boredom, or dishonesty. To enhance your voice tone, consider speaking at a reasonable speed, varying your pitch and loudness, and emphasizing your points with pauses and intonation. You may also work on your voice tone by recording yourself and listening to how it sounds.

Chapter 5: Navigating Small Talk with Ease

Transforming Casual Conversations into Meaningful Connections

Small chat is sometimes regarded as an essential but tedious aspect of socializing. It is the exchange of polite and superficial words like "How are you?" "What do you do?" and "How's the weather?" Small talk can help break the ice, fill silences, and strengthen social standards, but it can also be tedious, unpleasant, or pointless.

Small chat, on the other hand, does not have to be boring or superficial. Small talk may be a strong strategy for turning casual discussions into significant friendships.

You may accomplish the following by making effective small talk:

Demonstrate your interest and curiosity in the other person. - Establish trust and rapport by identifying common ground and shared experiences.

Share your thoughts and tales to express your personality and ideals.

Ask open-ended and follow-up questions to go deeper and more fascinating topics. - Make lasting and favorable impressions by being attentive, compassionate, and amusing.

Select relevant and interesting subjects for small conversation.

The topic chosen is an important aspect in determining the quality and direction of a conversation. Choosing a suitable and engaging topic for small talk might be the difference between a dull and awkward discussion and one that is dynamic and entertaining. Here are some suggestions for good small-talk topics:

Stay away from sensitive or contentious themes. Some topics should be avoided in small chat, especially with someone you don't know well or with whom you disagree. Politics, religion, money, health, and personal difficulties are examples of such themes.

These issues might elicit negative feelings, disagreements, or judgments, making the talk awkward or unpleasant. It is best to avoid certain issues until you are certain that the other person is open and eager to address them.

Select themes that are both current and timely. Choosing a topic that is relevant to the setting, person, or event is an excellent approach to starting a discussion. You can, for example, comment on the weather, the location, the cuisine, the music, or the speaker. You might also inquire about how the other person is doing, what brought them here, or what they are looking forward to. These subjects can help you connect with the other person and demonstrate your interest in the issue.

Choose subjects that are optimistic and uplifting. Another strategy to make a favorable impression and foster a pleasant atmosphere is to select topics that are optimistic and uplifting. You can, for example, discuss your interests, passions, objectives, successes, or plans. You may also inquire about the other person and convey your appreciation, interest, or support. These subjects can help you express your personality and ideals while also inspiring the other person to express theirs.

Select themes that are both common and relevant. Finally, consider themes that are common and relatable to both of you to keep the discussion going and develop rapport.

You can, for example, discuss family, friends, jobs, school, travel, or entertainment. You may also inquire about the other person and seek parallels, distinctions, or experiences. These themes can assist you in establishing common ground and shared experiences, as well as creating a sense of familiarity and trust.

To elicit more than yes or no replies, use open-ended and follow-up questions.

Asking open-ended and follow-up questions that elicit more than yes or no replies is one of the most successful methods to turn casual chat into meaningful connections.

Open-ended inquiries, such as "What do you think of...?" or "How do you feel about...?" or "What are some of the challenges that you face...?" request more than a simple yes or no answer. "Why do you say that?" "Can you tell me more about...?" or "How did you overcome...?" are examples of follow-up inquiries. You may aid yourself by asking open-ended and follow-up questions:

Express your curiosity and interest in the other person - Encourage the other person to give additional facts and insights

Dive further and more deeply into the issue - Show your knowledge and empathy - Invite the other person to ask you questions in return

Make use of the 5 Ws and 1 H. The 5 Ws and 1 H are simple techniques to produce open-ended questions: who, what, when, where, why, and how. Rather than asking, "Do you like your job?" ask, "What do you desire about your job?" or "How did you get into your field?" or "Who are some of the people you work with?" These inquiries can assist you in learning more about the other person's history, tastes, and experiences.

Apply the FORD technique. The FORD approach is another way to produce open-ended questions: family, occupation, leisure, and dreams. These are four broad and universal issues to which most people may connect and converse.

You may question, for example, "How is your family doing?", "What are some of the tasks you are working on?", "What do you like to do for fun?", and "What are some of your goals or aspirations?". These inquiries can assist you in learning about the other person's values, passions, and motivations.

Make use of the mirroring method. The mirroring approach, which involves repeating the last few words or phrases of the other person's answer and adding a question mark, is another way to produce open-ended queries.

If the other person replies, "I just returned from a trip to Italy," you might respond, "A trip to Italy?" This technique might help you demonstrate your attention and interest, encouraging the other person to expound on their answer.

Share your opinions and stories without being too self-centered or controversial.

Another way to transform small talk into meaningful connections is to share your opinions and stories without being too self-centered or controversial. Sharing your opinions and stories can help you:

- Express your personality and values
- Relate to the other person's emotions and understandings
- Add mixture and interest to the dialogue
- Invite the other person to share their opinions and stories

However, sharing your opinions and stories can also backfire if you are too self-centered or controversial. Being too self-centered means talking too much about yourself, without showing interest or respect for the other person. Being too controversial means expressing opinions that are offensive, insensitive, or divisive, without considering the other person's perspective or feelings. Here are some tips on how to share your opinions and stories effectively:

Use the 80/20 rule. A good balance between talking and listening is to follow the 80/20 rule: listen 80% of the time, and talk 20% of the time. This means that for every four sentences that the other person says, you say one sentence.

This will help you avoid dominating or interrupting the conversation and show that you are interested and attentive to the other person.

Use the sandwich technique. A good way to share your opinions without being too controversial is to use the sandwich technique: start with a positive or neutral statement, then state your opinion, and then end with another positive or neutral statement.

For example, instead of saying "I detest that movie, it was so boring and foolish", you can say "I'm pleased you enjoyed that movie, but I didn't like it very much, it was not my cup of tea". This technique can help you soften your opinion, acknowledge the other person's opinion, and avoid arguments or conflicts.

Use the STAR method. A good way to share your stories without being too self-centered is to use the STAR method: situation, task, action, and result. This is a simple and structured way to tell a story that is relevant, concise, and engaging. For example, instead of saying "I won a prize for my essay", you can say "I entered an essay contest about social issues, and I wrote about the impact of climate change on wildlife.

I did a lot of research and interviews, and I used some creative writing techniques. I was surprised and happy when I found out that I won the first prize". This method can help you provide context, details, and emotions to your story, and make the other person more interested and involved.

By applying these strategies and tips, you will be able to turn small talk into an enjoyable and rewarding experience and create lasting and meaningful connections with anyone you meet.

Finding Common Ground and Shared Interests.

Small conversations, however innocuous, maybe a powerful technique for connecting people. Those that cross-cultural, societal, and personal barriers. These fundamental touchpoints lay the groundwork for establishing common ground and creating a shared environment in which interactions may flourish.

The skill of finding common ground necessitates a keen knowledge of the situation and the people involved. The chapter discusses the significance of active listening in detecting signals and indications that indicate potential common interests.

Readers are urged to pay attention to nonverbal clues as well as words, encouraging a greater awareness of the tiny subtleties that might lead to the finding of common ground.

The ability to begin discussions that resonate with both parties is an important feature of handling small chats with chats. The chapter offers practical ways for directing talks toward neutral yet intriguing themes, allowing people to gradually discover mutual interests.

Readers learn to establish an environment conducive to the identification of common ground by asking open-ended questions and displaying genuine curiosity.

Throughout this chapter, the notion of reciprocity serves as a guiding principle. It underlines the significance of reciprocal participation and contribution to the debate. Readers are invited to openly discuss their interests, fostering an environment in which a spontaneous flow of ideas and experiences may develop. Individuals who do so establish a sense of connection that goes beyond the surface levels of small conversation.

Chapter 6: Active Listening and Responding

Developing the Skill of Active Listening

Active listening, like a perfectly tuned instrument in the hands of a skilled musician, is the foundation of effective communication. The capacity to actively listen becomes a transforming force as we traverse the complicated orchestration of human contact, establishing the framework for lasting connections.

Active listening is not a passive act in the communication symphony, but rather a conscious, dynamic interaction with the speaker.

The active listener goes beyond the basic reception of words, digging into the intricacies of tone, rhythm, and emotional complexity, driven by genuine interest and want to comprehend. This ability encompasses both the head and the heart, resulting in a harmonic confluence of receptivity and empathy.

The suspension of judgment is the first step in active listening. A skillful listener resists the need to generate replies while the speaker is expressing themselves. Instead, the listener enters a receptive state, allowing the speaker's words to be completely absorbed and understood. This act of nonjudgmental presence develops a climate of trust and openness, allowing for genuine expression.

The art of contemplation is the second movement. Like a mirror reflecting sunlight, the engaged listener articulates back the speaker's words, confirming their thoughts and emotions. This contemplation acts as both a confirmation of comprehension and a motivator for further investigation. It encourages the speaker to go further into their views, allowing for a more in-depth conversation.

The third movement entails recognizing nonverbal clues. While words provide specific meanings, gestures, attitudes, and postures weave a tapestry of communication. A good listener decodes nonverbal clues, focusing on the unsaid levels of communication.

This increased awareness deepens understanding, allowing the listener to absorb the entire scope of the speaker's message.

Responding arises as the ultimate conclusion in the crescendo of active listening. After absorbing the symphony of the speaker's expression, the engaged listener answers intelligently and sincerely. This comment is more than a reaction; it is a sophisticated addition to the continuing conversation. It demonstrates not just comprehension of the speaker's words, but also recognition of their feelings and points of view.

We go on a transforming journey as we practice active listening. Miscommunication becomes less of a cacophony, allowing for a more harmonic interchange in which individuals feel heard and understood. Active listening takes center stage in the great narrative of effective communication, arranging connections that reverberate long after the talk is over.

Formulating Thoughtful Responses

Understanding the complexities of active listening and reacting is analogous to learning the delicate ballet of verbal communication. It is critical to appreciate the enormous influence that our words may have on the quality of communication as we study the art of thoughtful answers.

Active listening, the foundation of good discourse, is a talent that extends beyond the auditory domain. It entails understanding not just the words said but also the underlying emotions, intentions, and unspoken subtleties. A skilled listener who is sensitive to both verbal and nonverbal signs is well-positioned to generate replies that are rich in depth and comprehension.

Thoughtful replies, at their core, are carefully prepared statements of comprehension and empathy. They demonstrate a profound connection with the speaker's message and are motivated by a genuine desire to connect.

The power of validation in answers is an important factor to consider. Recognizing the speaker's emotions and points of view helps the speaker feel heard and understood. Thoughtful comments go beyond just agreeing; they show regard for the speaker's unique perspective, building a mutual respect atmosphere.

Furthermore, this chapter delves into the technique of paraphrasing as a tool for confirming comprehension. We affirm comprehension while also providing a chance for clarification by rephrasing the speaker's words in our own. This approach improves overall communication quality by lowering the possibility of misunderstanding.

The astute communicator also understands the importance of nonverbal clues in response formulation. Facial expressions, body language, and subtle gestures all contribute to understanding unspoken language. Thus, thoughtful replies go beyond words to cover a more holistic representation of connection and participation.

The chapter also dives into the idea of empathy as a basis for meaningful answers. Understanding the speaker's feelings and ideas on a deeper level enables replies that are authentic and kind. This empathetic connection goes beyond surface-level exchanges, creating the basis for mutually beneficial partnerships.

In essence, the ability to formulate intelligent replies is an essential component of the wider skill set described by active listening. As we travel the landscape of discourse, let us not simply react, but design replies that resonate with the resonance of comprehension, empathy, and a real want to connect.

Chapter 7: Handling Difficult Conversations

Tackling Conflict with Diplomacy and Tact

Effective conflict resolution, like diagnosing a disease, begins with a thorough grasp of the underlying causes. It entails going beyond surface-level arguments to find the underlying causes and uncovering the emotions and views that contribute to the conflict. This portion of the diagnostic process necessitates a good observant eye, an empathic ear, and the capacity to notice subtle subtleties that are frequently missed by casual observers.

Once the diagnosis is established, the emphasis changes to developing a diplomatic solution. In this environment, diplomacy is about promoting mutual understanding and collaboration rather than about winning or losing. It entails approaching the discussion with an open mind, accepting opposing points of view, and seeking common ground. Just as a great physician tailors treatment plans to each particular patient, experienced communicators adapt their approach to each conflict's unique dynamics.

Tact, like a delicate surgical instrument, is required as we carry out the resolution approach.

It entails expressing assertively while remaining courteous, and carefully selecting words to minimize defensiveness and stimulate discourse. Tactful communication is a competent art that necessitates an awareness of the emotional sensitivities at work as well as the ability to conduct the conversation with grace. The objective is not to dominate, but rather to foster a climate in which all participants feel heard and appreciated.

Timing is crucial in the field of conflict resolution. Effective communicators choose appropriate periods for uncomfortable topics, just like a physician does when delivering a diagnosis.

They take into account the emotional states of those engaged, ensuring that talks take place when people are receptive and open to meaningful debate.

Furthermore, a preventative action comparable to health maintenance. Communicators can prevent disagreements from growing into larger problems by encouraging open lines of communication and resolving issues in their early stages. This proactive approach entails establishing a culture of transparency and trust in interpersonal connections.

Finally, mastering the skill of conducting tough talks necessitates a dedication to ongoing growth, similar to how a medical expert keeps up with the newest research and treatments. As communicators improve their diplomacy and tact, they not only effectively settle disagreements but also contribute to the general health and durability of their relationships. Difficult talks are transformed into chances for connection and understanding as a result of this method.

Turning Criticism into Constructive Dialogue

The sensitive terrain of challenging talks needs a sophisticated strategy that goes beyond simple verbal communication. As we learn how to turn criticism into constructive discourse, it is critical to realize the transforming potential of the constructive feedback loop.

Criticism, which is sometimes regarded as a discordant note in the symphony of communication, is, in reality, a crucial tool for personal and interpersonal development. It is a catalyst for refinement and progress rather than a destructive force. A fundamental part of handling such talks is to view them as chances for mutual understanding rather than conflicts.

Emotional intelligence takes center stage in the arena of productive discourse. Understanding both the criticizer and the criticized emotional undercurrents provides for a more empathic and deliberate reaction.

It is identifying the emotions at work, whether they be irritation, disappointment, or even terror, and reacting with a calm approach that creates a respectful environment.

Active listening is required for effective communication in the face of criticism. It entails not just listening to what is said but also interpreting the underlying concerns and intentions. By genuinely understanding the substance of the critique, one can answer with depth and honesty, addressing the base of the problem rather than just its surface manifestations.

Furthermore, the ability to ask clarifying questions becomes critical.

A competent communicator strives to untangle the layers of concern by offering questions that reveal the viewpoints of all parties concerned, especially in the context of criticism. This not only indicates a dedication to understanding but also allows the critics to express themselves more clearly.

Reframing becomes a strong tool in the transformative process of turning criticism into constructive discourse. Individuals are taught to consider criticism as a useful source of knowledge that promotes personal and professional progress rather than as a personal assault. By moving the narrative from blame to improvement, one may steer the debate in a more positive and solution-oriented direction.

Furthermore, a focus on collaborative problem-solving fosters the perception that all sides share a shared goal - improving the issue at hand. Engaging in a collaborative investigation of alternative solutions not only reduces stress but also fosters a feeling of togetherness in dealing with issues.

Mastering the art of transforming criticism into constructive discourse necessitates a comprehensive synthesis of emotional intelligence, active listening, and a collaborative mentality. Individuals may not only weather uncomfortable talks but also emerge from them with improved connections and a greater capacity for self-improvement if they embrace criticism as a catalyst for progress and react with empathy and awareness.

Chapter 8: Building Stronger Connections

Cultivating Authentic Relationships

Cultivating Authentic Relationships is similar to tending to a fragile garden, where the depth of connection blooms with deliberate care and attentive maintenance. The depth and sincerity of our connections are crucial in the arena of interpersonal dynamics, transcending basic social encounters to become foundations of emotional well-being and fulfillment.

Authenticity emerges as the basis upon which long-lasting interactions are created. Individuals must be sensitive to the emotional needs and vulnerabilities of others around them, just as a great gardener attends to the specific needs of each plant. This necessitates a commitment to be open, transparent, and honest with oneself, creating an atmosphere in which trust may take root and develop.

Empathy becomes the nutrient-rich soil that nurtures emotional attachments in the garden of true relationships. Individuals who have a true awareness of the viewpoints of others may manage the intricacies of human emotions with grace and compassion. We cultivate mutual understanding and shared experiences by carefully listening to and appreciating the sentiments of people with whom we contact. Communication, like the sunlight that nurtures the soil, is critical to establishing honesty.

Individuals feel seen and heard when they can express their opinions and emotions honestly while still recognizing the contributions of others. The exchange of ideas becomes a dance of reciprocity in which both parties contribute to the relationship's growth and enrichment.

Authentic relationships, like a garden rich with various flora, grow on acceptance and celebration of individual diversity. Accepting the differences in each person in our life gives brilliant colors to the fabric of connection. Relationships are enriched by a range of ideas, backgrounds, and personalities, just as a garden is more attractive with a variety of flowers.

Boundaries serve as a strong barrier that protects the growing garden of genuine friendships. Setting clear boundaries is an act of self-respect that fosters healthy and balanced relationships. Well-defined boundaries, like a well-tended garden where each plant has its own assigned place, offer a space for mutual growth without intruding on the originality of each member.

Finally, cultivating thankfulness acts as a continual flower in the garden of true connections. Expressing gratitude for the presence and contributions of others fosters a pleasant and reciprocal environment. Gratitude becomes a scent that pervades the air, leaving an unforgettable imprint on the hearts of those who participate in the dance of real connection.

In terms of strengthening bonds, cultivating honest relationships is a tribute to the beauty of human interaction. Individuals sow the seeds for relationships that last, grow, and beautify the landscape of their lives with enduring beauty as they tend to the delicate balance of authenticity, empathy, communication, acceptance, limits, and gratitude.

Networking Strategies for Professional and Personal Growth

Networking emerges as a potent driver for personal and professional success in the colorful environment of human contact. This phase serves as a guidepost, helping readers through the complexities of networking methods that not only create relationships but also pave the way for long-term success in both the professional and personal realms.

The Influence of Genuine Networking

Authentic networking stands out as a light of true involvement in a society overloaded with superficial relationships. This section underlines the significance of developing relationships based on sincerity and mutual gain.

Readers are urged to view networking as a chance to create genuine connections that will last the test of time, rather than a commercial exchange.

Using Digital Platforms

As the digital era reshapes the networking environment, this section delves into the strategic use of Internet platforms. From LinkedIn to professional forums, readers learn how to improve their digital profiles. The chapter provides practical advice on how to create an appealing online persona, engage in important debates, and use social media to grow their worldwide network.

Confidently Navigating Networking Events

Many people find networking gatherings intimidating. This section gives a road map for successfully navigating these meetings. Readers discover the intricacies that convert a networking gathering into a platform for creating important contacts, from mastering the art of introductions to gracefully quitting discussions.

Relationship Building Through Follow-Up

The chapter highlights that the essential core of networking is found in the follow-up, not the original connection. Readers learn the art of post-event interaction, including efficient email communication, social media connections, and the significance of keeping a regular presence to foster relationships over time.

Mentorship and mutual development
Mentorship emerges as a significant part of this reciprocity since networking is a two-way street. This section delves into the nature of mentor-mentee interactions, advising readers on how to properly seek and deliver mentorship. These ties become useful in personal and professional growth as a result of shared experiences and information sharing.

Overcoming Networking Difficulties
Networking is not without its difficulties, and this section discusses typical issues such as social anxiety and rejection dread.

Practical advice and tactics are presented to help readers overcome these obstacles, allowing them to approach networking with renewed vigor and confidence.

Maintaining Long-Term Relationships

The final chapter emphasizes the necessity of maintaining long-term relationships. Readers learn the value of regular check-ins, project cooperation, and celebrating their network's accomplishments. These activities transform connections into long-lasting partnerships that continue to fuel both personal and professional progress.

Chapter 9: Understanding Cultural Communication

Navigating Cross-Cultural Conversations

Language is only one aspect of cultural communication. It is a complicated interaction of conventions, traditions, social norms, and unspoken signs that vary amongst civilizations. It's a complicated dance in which each participant brings their beat, and the capacity to adapt to this diversity is critical.

We come across the notion of cultural intelligence as we go across the terrain of cross-cultural discussions.

It is not simply a matter of remembering a set of cultural rules, but of nurturing a true curiosity and respect for the ideals that underpin many nations. It entails changing our communication style without sacrificing sincerity, as well as creating an environment in which varied viewpoints may thrive.

Recognizing the effect of the environment is a major subject in understanding cultural communication. What is deemed proper or courteous in one culture may not be in another. Cultural sensitivity becomes a guiding principle, helping us to navigate interactions with grace and prevent unintended misunderstandings.

Furthermore, the chapter investigates prejudices and preconceived beliefs in cross-cultural encounters.

We can achieve real comprehension by recognizing and removing these prejudices. It's about breaking down assumptions and embracing the chance to learn from the wealth of experiences that each culture brings to the table.

The desire to listen and learn is a critical component of successful cross-cultural communication. Accepting different points of view broadens our awareness of the world and fosters a feeling of global citizenship. The chapter promotes respect for diverse ways of thinking and speaking by encouraging a paradigm change from ethnocentrism to cultural relativism.

From the importance of nonverbal communication indicators to altering communication techniques based on cultural expectations, practical solutions for handling cross-cultural talks are also revealed. The objective is not to standardize communication, but to increase our adaptability and suppleness, so that talks become bridges rather than walls.

Understanding cultural communication is a necessary ability in an increasingly linked world. It's about appreciating the beauty in our diversity and using it to foster growth and connection.

We equip ourselves not just with the means to communicate successfully, but also with the capacity to establish meaningful relationships that overcome cultural barriers as we negotiate the complicated web of cross-cultural talks.

Respecting and Embracing Diversity

Respecting and appreciating cultural variety is analogous to studying the rich and various languages of a global symphony. Our planet is a colorful tapestry of civilizations, each adding its distinctive note to humanity's collective music. To master the art of conversation, one must grasp the complex harmonies of cross-cultural communication.

Begin by appreciating the beauty of diversity. Cultural cues enrich our relationships, providing richness and texture to the conversational canvas. Each culture carries with it its own set of values, customs, and opinions. Accepting variety opens opportunities for understanding and fosters friendships that cross geographical borders.

Language, as a pillar of cultural identity, is crucial in communication. It contains the essence of a culture's history and worldview beyond simple words. Understanding the nuances of language allows for a more meaningful relationship.

Linguistic awareness is essential for bridging cultural barriers, whether it's recognizing the significance of a certain greeting or comprehending the cultural meanings of certain terms.

In cross-cultural relationships, nonverbal communication takes center stage. Across civilizations, the unwritten language of gestures, facial expressions, and body language differs greatly. Sensitivity to these cues promotes deeper comprehension, allowing people to connect not just with words, but also with the silent language of shared movements and expressions.

Cultural communication is a dynamic dance of similarity and diversity.

Finding common ground while honoring differences is an art form. It necessitates a desire to leave one's cultural comfort zone and embrace the unexpected with an open heart and mind. Conversations become a celebration of difference as a result, creating an environment in which each person feels seen and heard.

Understanding cultural communication is more than just knowing the basics. It entails a lifelong fascination with the history, customs, and social forces that form a culture. To have a more inclusive and enjoyable conversation experience, ask questions, listen carefully, and engage in cultural exchange with real curiosity.

Cultural sensitivity is a key tool in professional dealings. Business transcends borders, and excellent cross-cultural communication is critical to success. Recognizing and valuing the many approaches to negotiation, decision-making, and collaboration that different cultures take fosters trust and rapport on the global stage.

Finally, embracing diversity in cultural communication is more than just a topic of discussion; it is a mindset that defines how we interact with others. Individuals contribute to a global discussion that embraces the diversity of human experience by weaving threads of cultural understanding into the fabric of communication.

Chapter 10: Mastering Digital Communication

Effective Communication in the Age of Technology

The throbbing heartbeat of communication echoes across the conduits of technology in our modern world, ushering in an era in which digital interactions are as pervasive as the air we breathe.

With its diverse platforms and channels, the digital sphere presents both possibilities and problems. This reveals the broad panorama of digital communication, from emails to instant messaging, and social media to video conferencing.

It teaches readers to recognize the distinct characteristics that each platform possesses, highlighting the significance of customizing one's approach to the medium.

This becomes a guide through the labyrinth of unwritten standards by addressing the digital etiquette that regulates online communications. It reveals the complexities of tone in digital communication, encouraging readers to use their words carefully to communicate intended meanings in the absence of voice nuances or facial emotions.

Readers are encouraged to investigate the complexities of virtual presence as the story progresses.

The phase reveals the skill of building a digital identity that connects with clarity and honesty, from crafting an engaging online presence to presenting authenticity via a screen. It addresses the delicate balance between professionalism and personal expression, advising readers on how to walk the narrow line with grace.

It explores the possible problems of misinterpretation in a future where messages travel at the speed of light throughout the digital sphere. Readers are given techniques for decoding confusing communications, promoting digital literacy that extends beyond the surface of pixels and bytes.

A substantial amount of the chapter is devoted to the art of virtual meetings and conferences, which are an essential component of modern professional communication. The chapter presents a road map for transforming digital meetings into collaborative and productive experiences, from grasping the complexities of video conferencing systems to promoting involvement in virtual locations.

The chapter does not overlook the role of mindfulness in digital communication in the middle of the technological tapestry. It urges readers to be aware of their digital imprint, encouraging a culture of courteous and responsible engagement that extends beyond the bounds of the virtual world.

Navigating Virtual Conversations and Online Presence

It encourages readers to analyze the peculiar dynamics of virtual talks, where the lack of tangible indicators necessitates a greater sensitivity to language, tone, and context. Mastering digital communication requires an acute awareness of the details that affect our online engagements, whether through email conversations, video conferencing, or social media connections.

Individuals are urged to construct a digital identity that coincides with their personal and professional aspirations in a world where first impressions are typically established through a screen.

Navigating internet communications also necessitates a thorough awareness of the ever-changing environment of online etiquette. Readers are taken through the hidden laws that govern the digital sphere, from the subtleties of email conversation to the complexities of participation in virtual meetings. The chapter dives into the dos and don'ts of online engagement, offering practical advice to assist people in navigating the virtual environment with confidence and professionalism.

Furthermore, the chapter investigates the effect of digital communication in developing relationships and network creation.

It dives into the value of social media as a networking tool, highlighting the need to build meaningful virtual connections. From LinkedIn to Twitter, readers will learn how to use online platforms to develop their professional networks and advance their careers.

In an age where attention spans are short and information overload is common, the chapter finishes by discussing the art of brief and powerful digital communication. Readers are instructed on how to improve their capacity to communicate messages effectively and convincingly, ensuring that their online encounters make a lasting impact.

Conclusion

Sustaining Lifelong Communication Skills

It is critical to recognize that the art of communication is not a static talent that can be acquired and then put away. Instead, it is a dynamic and ever-changing discipline that needs ongoing cultivation. Maintaining lifetime communication skills necessitates a continual commitment to self-reflection and adaptation.

The end underlines the significance of incorporating gained knowledge into daily living.

Readers are advised to make intentional attempts to implement the ideas gained in a variety of situations, such as personal relationships, professional settings, or casual interactions. As a result, the techniques learned throughout the book become engrained in the reader's natural communication style.

Recognizing that progress frequently comes from discomfort is an important part of maintaining lifelong communication skills. The end encourages readers to view difficult tasks as chances for growth and learning. Just as effort grows a muscle, so does communication ability when confronted with the intricacies of conflicting viewpoints and perspectives.

Furthermore, the conclusion emphasizes the need to be receptive to input. Constructive criticism becomes a vital refining tool, helping individuals to recognize areas for growth and adjust their communication approach accordingly. Readers establish the groundwork for a lifetime of productive and meaningful communication by cultivating an attitude of continuous learning.

The book also urges readers to try new things to broaden their expressive horizons. The conclusion calls for a proactive approach to skill building, which includes anything from joining discussion groups to attending workshops and seminars. It implies that lifelong learners are people who seek chances to improve and increase their communication toolset.

www.ingramcontent.com/pod-product-compliance
Lightning Source LLC
Chambersburg PA
CBHW062326290526

45794CB00005B/1920